An opini

FREE LONDON

Written by
Emmy Watts

God's Own Junkyard (no.29)

INFORMATION IS DEAD.
LONG LIVE OPINION.

This book is useless. If you really want to save money then just go online, find out what's free in the capital and do that.

Not quite! Your hard-earned cash is well spent on this book. While you may find plenty of information in the dark recesses of the internet, you can't find the glorious, shiny opinion contained within these pages. This is your lively, compact guide to all you need to know about having a seriously good, seriously interesting and, in these cost-of-living-challenged days, a seriously free time in the world's greatest capital city.

Other opinionated guides:

East London	*Sweet London*
London Architecture	*Kids' London*
Vegan London	*Escape London*
London Green Spaces	*Eco London*
Independent London	*Big Kids' London*
London Pubs	*Art London*

The Garden at 120 (no. 18)

This page: BAPS Shri Swaminarayan Mandir (no.24)
Opposite: Sir John Soane's Museum (no.4)

This page: Hampstead Heath (no.19)
Opposite: Crystal Palace Park (no.42)

THE BEST THINGS IN ~~LIFE~~ LONDON ARE FREE

Believe it or not, living on a shoestring and enjoying the greatest city in the world are not mutually exclusive concepts. Pigs will not fly, hell will not freeze over, and you won't be tempted to take out a payday loan. Don't believe us? Well, we made a book to prove you wrong. A book so packed with (sometimes) weird and (universally) wonderful ideas for wallet-friendly London outings, you'll wonder what on earth you did without it.

London is internationally famed for its free museums and galleries. In fact, there are so many great free archives filled with unique objects, paintings and manuscripts on such a staggering array of themes, we could have written the whole book just on those. In the interest of variety, however, we narrowed it down to our all-time favourites: from national collections to quirky house museums, and threw in loads of other complimentary culture to boot, from pioneering art galleries to riotous free gigs – none of which require so much as a wink in the doorman's direction to gain access.

And then there's parks. Lovely, vital, verdant parks. It might sound obvious, but the majority of London's green spaces are totally free to visit. Given that they cover a fifth of the city, that's actually pretty incredible. We're not talking your standard scruffy scrap of grass either. There are wild, ancient parklands, impeccably manicured royal gardens, leafy lunch spots blooming from bombed-out ruins, and even rooftop gardens towering 15 storeys above street level.

And what about learning opportunities? Take LSE's programme of illuminating public lectures (no.3), which are open to all and cover topics as diverse as anthropology and gender studies. Or Tara Yoga's tri-weekly hatha meets (no.9), where you can learn your happy baby from your downward-facing dog, without the inflated gym fees.

What might surprise you most about this book is the number of places in it that you'd probably assumed were closed to the public. Did you know that you can turn up at The Old Bailey (no.1) without warning and watch a murder trial unfold? Or get a tour of the magnificent Neasden Temple (no.24) any day of the week? You could even rock up at the Palace of Westminster (no.59) and catch an impassioned debate without having to open your wallet.

And if that all sounds brilliant, well, they do say the best things in life are free. We'd argue that the best things in London are free too. Not necessarily because they're the most entertaining (though they often are), but because their freeness is so often the result of selflessness and generosity – on the part of Londoners alive and kicking, and those long gone. While we all love getting something for nothing, many of these experiences offer an opportunity to give something back, whether it's helping to keep the justice system accountable, offering precious encouragement as a member of the audience or even just being a part of something bigger than ourselves. So, the next time you head out, do yourself a favour and leave your card at home, disable Google Pay, and embrace the free(dom).

Emmy Watts, London 2023

BEST FOR...

Grand days out

Got time on your side? Explore Hampstead Heath's (no.19) untamed charms and its crowning jewel, the magnificent Kenwood House (no.22). Meanwhile in east London, The Line (no.36) art walk connects 22 thought-provoking sculptures along a five-mile route and makes the perfect weekend outing when combined with the haunting Longplayer sound installation (no.34).

Cultural activities

Art doesn't get much fresher than NOW Gallery's (no.37) trailblazing installations, with past offerings including a patterned labyrinth and a huge inhabitable sweater. At the other end of the art historical spectrum, the elegant Guildhall Art Gallery (no.6) is home to an impressive hoard of paintings dating from 1670. Oh, and there's a Roman amphitheatre in the basement.

Catching up with friends

Lazy weekend get-togethers call for a relaxed amble around the (literal) concrete jungle that is the Barbican Conservatory (no.13), where you can set the world to rights in the company of 1,500 species of plants. Fancy something higher octane? Round up your mates, strap on your skates, and join the Friday Night Skate and Sunday Stroll collective (no.54) on an exhilarating cross-capital tour.

Classes and workshops

Learning doesn't have to cost an arm and a leg. Gresham College (no.8) hosts free lectures by eminent academics every week, with topics as varied as art, astronomy and ancient history. Or, if it's inner harmony you're after, Inner Space's (no.10) weekly in-person meditation sessions are open to all and will restore your zen in minutes.

Green escapes

When city living starts to give you a headache, abscond to one of the capital's iconic green spaces. Favourite spots include the leafy Parkland Walk (no.23), a three-mile linear park tracing the route of a long-gone railway; and the 600 tranquil acres that make up Hyde Park and Kensington Gardens (no.52).

Family outings

With its drop-in children's workshops, digital drawing gallery and endless scampering space, Tate Modern (no.39) is one of the best free family hangouts (and the art isn't bad either). On fairer weather days, grab a picnic and head to Crystal Palace Park (no.42) in search of its colossal hedgerow maze and herd of full-scale model dinosaurs.

Date night

They might not sound that romantic, but the Old Blue Last's (no.5) rowdy free gigs offer some of the best after-dark entertainment you can get in this city. Or if a sticky-floored dive bar isn't their thing, let St Paul's (no.14) world-famous choir serenade them at an awe-inspiring Evensong service.

SEASONAL EVENTS

LONDON NEW YEAR'S DAY PARADE

If you're not nursing a hangover, then cheering on a procession of brass bands and pearly kings and queens is the only sensible way to spend New Year's Day. Simply select a vantage point between Piccadilly and the Palace of Westminster.

Winter | lnydp.com

LUNAR NEW YEAR IN CHINATOWN

The start of the lunar calendar is celebrated all over the capital, but no one does lanterns and lion dances quite like Chinatown. Get there early to snag a spot on the parade route, before heading to Trafalgar Square for the thrilling firework finale.

Winter | chinatown.co.uk

PRIDE IN LONDON

This glorious celebration has been drawing LGBTQ+ folks and their allies to Soho since 1972, and now attracts more than a million revellers. With its spectacular parade and incredible sense of community, it truly is something to be proud of.

Summer | prideinlondon.org

NOTTING HILL CARNIVAL

Each August Bank Holiday, this celebration of Caribbean culture lures two million colourfully clad pleasure seekers to west London for two days of dancing, banging tunes and an extremely feather-heavy street parade.

Summer | nhcarnival.org

FRIEZE SCULPTURE

While Frieze isn't known for its affordability, the art fair's open-air counterpart is free to all, exhibiting sculpture by the world's most exciting artists in the tranquil surrounds of Regent's Park. Download the audio guide for insights from curator Clare Lilley.

Autumn | frieze.com

LONDON DESIGN FESTIVAL

Every September, LDF spends nine days proving London's standing as a design capital of the world. The line-up is jam-packed with pioneering installations and hands-on workshops, so check the website for highlights before you head out.

Autumn | londondesignfestival.com

OPEN HOUSE

For two weeks every year, hundreds of (mostly) private buildings welcome the architecturally interested (or just plain nosy) public. Everywhere from Trellick Tower to Stockwell Garage is open, but spaces go quickly so act fast to avoid disappointment.

Autumn | open-city.org.uk

RIDELONDON FREECYCLE

You don't need to be the next Bradley Wiggins to take part in this eight-mile bike ride. In fact, rookies are actively welcomed – and with live music, complimentary snacks and the route closed to traffic, there's really no excuse not to get on your bike.

Spring | ridelondon.co.uk

1

OLD BAILEY TRIAL

True crime, as it happens

Maybe it's the Old Bailey's gruesome history (and hopefully not because you've recently committed a murder), but you can't help but feel a sense of trepidation when wandering its infamous halls. In fact, even observing a case as a bystander with zero vested interest can still feel a little nerve-wracking. But, aside from doing your bit to help keep the justice system honest, why do it? Well, watching a real-life trial unfold in real time can be more absorbing than even the biggest-budget blockbuster. In fact, it might just be one of the most enthralling experiences of your life. No popcorn in court though. Sorry.

Old Bailey, EC4M 7EH
Nearest station: St Paul's
cityoflondon.gov.uk

2

BRITISH MUSEUM

Vast showcase of culture

Few things are so unappealing to the seasoned Londoner as battling crowds of tourists at the capital's largest museum, but a browse around this archaeological dreamland might just be worth the fight. While embarrassingly few artefacts in the BM were either made or found in Britain – the majority having been acquired as the result of colonial exploitation during the age of empire – you have to admit that this is one hell of a hoard. The Rosetta Stone, mummies and Parthenon sculptures are obviously must-sees, while the enlightening 'LGBTQ Histories' and 'Collecting and Empire' trails lend intriguing context to ancient relics.

Great Russell Street, WC1B 3DG
Nearest stations: Tottenham Court Road, Russell Square
britishmuseum.org

3

LSE PUBLIC LECTURES

Money matters (and other subjects)

That the LSE has spawned more billionaires than any other European university may be reason enough to attend one of its regular free lectures – especially if you're reading this book. Then again, there are probably quicker ways to make money than rocking up to the odd chat about fiscal policy. So, instead, head here for the inspiring professors, eminent guest speakers, grand lecture theatres and variety of talks covering everything from accounting and statistics to anthropology and gender studies – plus the opportunity to relive those heady student years. Yep, it turns out economics isn't quite the yawn-fest we'd imagined.

32 Lincoln's Inn Fields, WC2A 3PH
Nearest station: Holborn
lse.ac.uk

4

SIR JOHN SOANE'S MUSEUM

Holborn home of the maximalist architect

That you're forced to decant your possessions into a transparent carrier bag before setting foot inside the museum is the first clue that this place is – to put it mildly – a bit eccentric. But cross the threshold of this confounding Tardis, and the bag actually makes a lot of sense. Impossibly narrow corridors, illuminating light shafts and hidden alcoves impart a disorienting effect that doesn't always mix with Soane's vast collection of precariously displayed archaeological artefacts. Still, by the time the labyrinthine one-way system spits you back out onto the street, you'll no doubt be convinced that more is most definitely more (except when it comes to entry fees, anyway).

13 Lincoln's Inn Fields, WC2A 3BP
Nearest station: Holborn
soane.org

5

THE OLD BLUE LAST FREE GIGS

Lively performances at a charismatic venue

At first glance, this sparse and moody East End boozer doesn't feel like much to write home about. Ascend the stairs and encounter its infamous Live Room on a gig night, however, and – well, it's probably best you *don't* write home about that. Indeed, what this historic watering hole disregards in terms of soft furnishings and Sunday roasts, it more than makes up for with its infamously riotous music events, which cover everything from acoustic sets and indie nights to album launches and themed parties. Many of these are free and any of them could get messy (it is, after all, owned by VICE), so dress down, pack your earplugs, and don't say we didn't warn you.

38 Great Eastern Street, EC2A 3ES
Nearest station: Shoreditch High Street
Book in advance
theoldbluelast.com

6

GUILDHALL ART GALLERY

Romantic art and Roman remains

This City of London gallery is architecturally stunning, historically significant, free to access and *woefully* underrated, with footfall considerably lower than that of similar museums. This would be scandalous enough were its 4,500-strong collection of artworks – comprising haunting pieces by Rossetti and Millais as well as the best array of cityscapes we've ever laid eyes on – the only string to its bow, but this house of treasures is hiding something even more extraordinary in its basement: namely the illuminated remains of London's only Roman amphitheatre. Add exhibitions, family workshops and guided tours to the list of freebies, and there's absolutely no reason why this shouldn't be one of London's most visited museums.

Basinghall Street, EC2V 5AE
Nearest station: Bank
cityoflondon.gov.uk

7

THE NATIONAL GALLERY

Arresting A-Z of art history

No matter how thronged with culture-hungry tourists, the National still manages to be one of the most peaceful spots in the capital. Indeed, the sheer volume of masterpieces in its permanent collection seems to stun the gallery's daily hordes into awe-struck silence, as though spellbound by Vermeer's soulful stares and Van Gogh's dreamlike skies. The free galleries are encyclopaedic in scope, but supposing you don't have time to work your way through every artist, you can take one of three speedy – though no less spectacular – art routes, so you can glimpse a Canaletto on your coffee break or a Leonardo on your lunch.

Trafalgar Square, WC2N 5DN
Nearest station: Charing Cross
nationalgallery.org.uk

8

GRESHAM COLLEGE LECTURES

Degree-level learning without the fees

Got a thirst for knowledge (but no funds for college)? This charming institution might just be the City of London's best-kept secret, quietly offering free lectures to anyone who wants to learn for more than 400 years. While we're not suggesting that an ad hoc programme of talks on wildly disparate subjects is any match for a formal university education, the sheer variety of subjects covered by Gresham's lively lecturers should at the very least give you an edge when it comes to the local pub quiz. And if that's not enough, the setting – a 13th-century oak-panelled hall accessed through a clandestine tunnel – will have you feeling every inch the Oxbridge scholar.

Barnard's Inn, EC1N 2HH
Nearest station: Chancery Lane
Book in advance
gresham.ac.uk

9

HATHA YOGA AT TARA YOGA CENTRE

Mindful posing, guaranteed dozing

Seeking spiritual and corporeal nirvana? An unassuming backstreet off the Old Street roundabout might not be the most likely place to find it, but Tara Yoga's free thrice-weekly classes are so blissfully transportive they could take place almost anywhere and still lift you to a higher plane. While classes vary in focus depending on the day, the end result – namely a state of total tranquillity – is largely the same. In fact, come the end-of-session relaxation, don't be surprised to hear satisfied snores emanating from neighbouring mats (that is, if you haven't already nodded off).

25-31 Ironmonger Row, EC1V 3QW
Nearest station: Old Street
Book in advance
tarayogacentre.co.uk

10

INNER SPACE

Midweek mindfulness

A trip into Zone 1 can be traumatic at the best of times, and yet few people seem aware that there's a cure for crowd-induced migraines tucked away in a Covent Garden basement. Once a week, Inner Space's trained volunteers whisper away your worries during a free 20-minute lunchtime meditation, leaving you relaxed, recharged and ready to re-join the hubbub above. Those who can't make the in-person session are welcome to tune in to the daily online offering, though it's worth popping by to make use of the pink-tinged, tranquil and free-to-access meditation room the next time you're in town.

36 Short's Gardens, WC2H 9AB
Nearest station: Covent Garden
Book in advance
innerspace.org.uk

11

GRANT MUSEUM OF ZOOLOGY

UCL's morbid menagerie

What this diminutive museum lacks in square footage, it makes up for in pretty much everything else. Buckets of character? *Check*. Free entry? *Check*. One of the weirdest collections of objects you've ever laid eyes on? Well, unless you routinely ogle tightly-packed jars of moles and disembowelled monkeys, then *check*. And while hanging out in a room full of corpses might sound like a decidedly miserable way to pass an hour, the Grant's 67,000-strong collection of skeletal, soused and/or squashed specimens is actually eerily beautiful and unexpectedly life-affirming – once you get over the initial ick.

Rockefeller Building, 21 University Street, WC1E 6DE
Nearest station: Euston Square
ucl.ac.uk

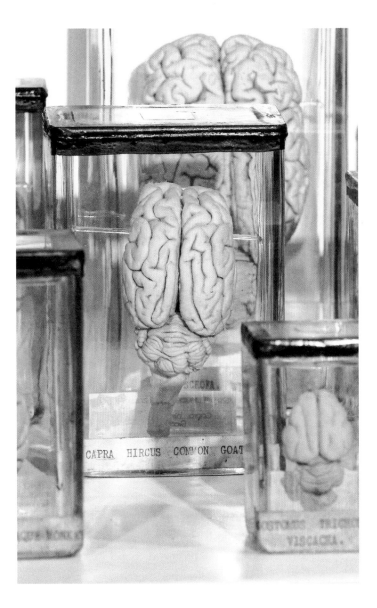

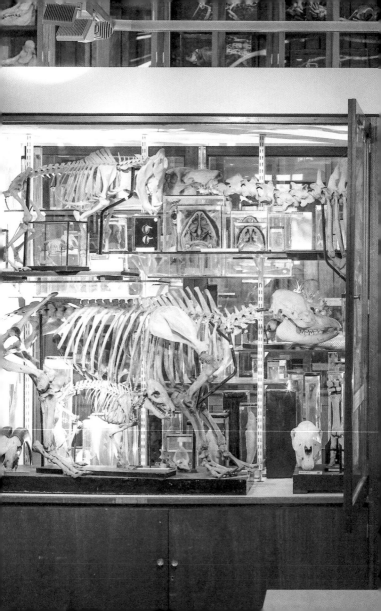

12

ST DUNSTAN
IN THE EAST

Leafy park in sacred ruins

When the City feels like a soulless, grasping void, seek out this eerie Eden emerging from the ruins of a bomb-ravaged church. The hapless victim of both the Great Fire of London and the Blitz, this open-access paradise serves as a monument to the area's unfortunate past, as well as a spooky glimpse into a possible post-apocalyptic future, where vines snake up stone walls, trees thrust through empty windows and a carpet of moss buries all trace of humanity. Today though, it's just a really lovely place to eat your sandwiches.

St Dunstan's Hill, EC3R 5DD
Nearest station: Monument
cityoflondon.gov.uk

13

BARBICAN CONSERVATORY

The original concrete jungle

When you're craving some greenery but the weather has other ideas, head to the Barbican's indoor rainforest – a leafy paradise that's home to more than 1,500 species of plants, many rare and endangered. Despite being London's second-largest conservatory (the largest is the Palm House at Kew), this Brutalist beauty can sometimes feel claustrophobic with its gyrating TikTokers and slow-moving weekend crowds – an inevitability of limited opening hours. But don't be deterred; thanks to its cute resident terrapins, free audio trail and Hanging Gardens of Babylon vibes, a mooch around the conservatory is still one of the capital's top Sunday pastimes, and infinitely more interesting than a stroll in the park.

Silk Street, EC2Y 8DS
Nearest station: Moorgate
Book in advance
barbican.org.uk

14

EVENSONG AT
ST PAUL'S CATHEDRAL

Stirring sung prayer services

While faith is not a prerequisite for enjoying St Paul's daily service of sung prayer, a willingness to suspend your disbelief for 45 minutes probably should be. Indeed, whatever your convictions, it's hard to accept that the legendary choir's angelic voices are anything less than heaven-sent – their harmonies so powerful they lift the soul and dispel all mortal worries (at least temporarily). You won't be able to see inside the crypt or dome (for that, you'll need a paid ticket) but you will be sitting in the cathedral's impressive nave. And if all that other-worldliness sounds a little out of your comfort zone, try the earthy Sunday organ recitals for all the restful vibes minus the amens and hallelujahs.

St Paul's Churchyard, EC4M 8AD
Nearest station: St Paul's
stpauls.co.uk

15

LONDON MITHRAEUM

Archaeological attraction under contemporary lens

It seems like everything is an immersive experience now, to the point where even the remains of a third-century Roman temple – recently opened as a public exhibit in Bloomberg's glossy City headquarters – has been given the 21st-century treatment. The experience lasts just under 20 minutes and requires visitors to assemble around the temple ruins and observe as it is 'brought to life' by hypnotic light projections and enigmatic sound effects. Sure, it's an impressive spectacle, but the stupendousness of what you are actually looking at – namely one of the most significant archaeological discoveries in London – is somewhat lost in the haze. Still well worth a look though.

12 Walbrook, EC4N 8AA
Nearest station: Cannon Street
Book in advance
londonmithraeum.com

16

ARCHITECTURAL ASSOCIATION PUBLIC PROGRAMME

Enlightening talks at eminent design school

Fancy yourself as the next Zaha Hadid? Then why not fill up on free architectural wisdom at the institution where she cut her teeth? While the AA's prestigious reputation and majestic Georgian frontage may feel intimidating, its public lectures are anything but, offering everyone from master architects to the creatively clueless illuminating (and pleasingly jargon-free) insights into the world of design and construction. Head in-house for access to leading architects, lively post-lecture debates and the odd drinks reception, or check out the live stream for talks on everything from playground planning to sustainable development from the comfort of your couch.

36 Bedford Square, WC1B 3ES
Nearest station: Tottenham Court Road
Book in advance
aaschool.ac.uk

17

LIVE AT LUNCH AT THE ROYAL OPERA HOUSE

Lunch-break pirouettes and piano duets

This Covent Garden institution is so illustrious, tickets to its productions so sought-after, it likely never occurred to you that you might be able to swing by on your lunch break and catch a world-class performance for absolutely nothing. Well, you can. Every Friday, artists from the Royal Opera, Royal Ballet and in-house orchestra will trill, twirl and toot your workweek frustrations into dust in the sun-drenched Paul Hamlyn Hall. The best bit? It's so relaxed you can turn up in track pants and trainers with a thumping hangover and no one will bat an eyelid – just pray they haven't scheduled a soprano to belt out *The Magic Flute*.

Bow Street, WC2E 9DD
Nearest station: Covent Garden
roh.org.uk

18

THE GARDEN AT 120

Serenity among the skyscrapers

While the City of London's largest roof garden is far from its most dizzying at just 15 floors up, this rooftop refuge still boasts some of the area's most dramatic views from its midway vantage point. Snugly sandwiched between the Gherkin and Walkie Talkie buildings, the glass-walled, open-air viewing platform offers exceptional close-ups of London's most architecturally noteworthy buildings, as well as 360-degree vistas stretching across the capital and beyond. Views aside, the garden's relaxing water feature and lush landscaping mean it's simply a really nice spot to spend time in, whether you're planning a sky-high proposal or just looking to 'elevate' your lunch break.

120 Fenchurch Street, EC3M 5BA
Nearest station: Fenchurch Street, Monument
thegardenat120.com

19

HAMPSTEAD HEATH

An ancient and rambling countryside escape

Nature's greatest gift to north Londoners boasts 800 acres of gorgeously moody parkland, a gloriously grisly 1,000-year history and unsurpassed views of the London skyline from the lofty summit at Parliament Hill. A former stomping ground of Keats, Coleridge, Constable et al., the enigmatic Heath has inspired some of the world's greatest works of art, and it's not hard to see why. Dramatic scenery, chance encounters with wildlife, fairy-tale follies in hidden gardens and winding walks are just a few of this ancient wonder's complimentary offerings. Be warned though, visit the Heath once and it will likely steal your heart (otherwise, it's totally free).

Nearest stations: Hampstead Heath, Gospel Oak
cityoflondon.gov.uk

20

ABNEY PARK CEMETERY

Rebels' resting place

Cemeteries don't get more radical than Abney Park, the 'Magnificent Seven' boneyard famed for being the final resting place of many of London's religious dissenters. Like its sister sites across the city, the Stoke Newington sanctuary is modelled on iconic Paris necropolis Père Lachaise, though its haphazard arrangement of dead-end paths, chaotically plonked monuments, crumbling gravestones and a gorgeously gothic non-denominational chapel – the first of its kind in Europe – make it that bit wilder than majestic Brompton or theatrical Highgate.

215 Stoke Newington High Street, N16 0LH
Nearest station: Stoke Newington
abneypark.org

21

UCL OBSERVATORY

Barnet's star attraction

In need of some serious escapism? Enter UCL's UFO-like teaching observatory – an unearthly palace of astronomy that, while generally reserved for its researchers and students, opens its gleaming silver domes to the public twice a month. Despite being almost a century old, this Mill Hill marvel is said to be one of the best spots in the country to stargaze, with all aspiring astronomers permitted to peer through the facility's Fry 8-inch refractor, provided there's a clear view. And if there isn't? A tour of the intriguing facilities still makes for a stellar night out.

553 Watford Way, Mill Hill, NW3 2QS
Nearest station: Mill Hill East
Book in advance
ucl.ac.uk

22

KENWOOD HOUSE

Striking villa on the edge of Hampstead Heath

With its imposing setting, prestigious art collection and (neo)classical good looks, this stucco-fronted mansion could easily feel a little intimidating. Fortunately for its loyal fan base of muddy-booted hikers though, a mooch around Kenwood is easily one of London's most comforting weekend activities, with eternal free entry thanks to a hefty bequest by its former owner and a family-friendly feel courtesy of current owner English Heritage. So, make yourself at home in the Robert Adam-designed library and get as close to treasured paintings by Vermeer and Gainsborough as you like – but perhaps remember to scrape those wellies first.

Hampstead Lane, NW3 7JR
Nearest station: Highgate
Book in advance
english-heritage.org.uk

23

PARKLAND WALK

5km park on old railway tracks

Abandoned train stations. A bat sanctuary. A giant sculpture of a creeping Cornish fairy-tale *spriggan*. The Parkland Walk's constituent parts might sound like the stuff of nightmares, but put them together and you've got one of London's most beautiful – if occasionally creepy – perambulations. Following the route of a disused railway line, Britain's longest nature reserve runs from Ally Pally in the north down to the western end of Finsbury Park, with a break in the middle to cross through Highgate. Short on time? The bottom half is infinitely more interesting than the top, boasting vibrant street art, the exhilarating Cape Adventure Playground and, for better or worse, that bloody spriggan.

Nearest stations: Highgate, Finsbury Park
parkland-walk.org.uk

24

BAPS SHRI SWAMINARAYAN MANDIR

Traditional Hindu stone temple

The 'Neasden Temple' feels too casual a moniker for such a grand building, and yet this marble marvel's laidback alias somehow sets the tone for what's to come. Everyone is free to enter the mandir, regardless of spiritual inclination, and all are warmly welcomed by its knowledgeable *swamis* (monks), who will keenly impart their seemingly boundless wisdom – however loose your handle on Hinduism. There's so much to see and it's easy to miss bits, so plan ahead, check the *arti* (ritual) times and leave extra time to explore the breathtaking grounds.

Pramukh Swami Road, NW10 8HW
Nearest station: Neasden
londonmandir.baps.org

25

ROYAL ACADEMY OF MUSIC

Rousing recitals at a celebrated conservatoire

As hobbies go, classical music appreciation isn't renowned for its affordability, but Bach buffs on a budget needn't despair: this 200-year-old conservatoire's packed programme of free events means a bulging bank account isn't a precondition for a full cultural calendar. While it might lack the ceremony of more formal venues, there's a singular magic in ascending the Academy's well-trodden steps, scaled by a chorus of famed alumni, and witnessing future superstars in their incubation. Free performances are generally small – expect intimate sonatas and cosy chamber works – but the students' genius is undeniable, and the sheer variety of what's on offer will be music to your ears.

Marylebone Road, NW1 5HT
Nearest station: Baker Street
Book in advance
ram.ac.uk

26

WELLCOME COLLECTION

Thought-provoking medical museum

Its position on roaring Euston Road makes this shrine to science easy to saunter past, despite the fact that it's massive (located within the headquarters of the Wellcome Trust – the world's third-richest charity) and stuffed with all manner of treasures. Founded at the bequest of Henry Wellcome, famed as the architect of the modern pharmaceutical industry, the museum maintains a tireless commitment to showcasing cutting-edge advancements in medicine with its ever-changing programme of fun and futuristic exhibits. And if you're seeking a central London workspace, it doesn't get quieter, cosier or altogether lovelier than the tranquil third-floor Reading Room.

183 Euston Road, NW1 2BE
Nearest station: Euston
wellcomecollection.org

27

BRITISH LIBRARY

Literary nirvana on Euston Road

It might be the largest public building constructed in the UK in the 20th century, but this red-brick goliath can feel impenetrable with its book-preserving windowless walls and rumours of Reader Pass exclusivity. In reality, it's one of London's friendlier libraries, and pretty much anyone can snag a pass, whether they're studying for a PhD in astrophysics or just fancy a browse through the *Beano*'s back catalogue (or any one of the BL's 200 million other publications). Overwhelmed by choice? Make a beeline for the Treasures Gallery, where highlights spanning original Beatles manuscripts and childhood works by the Brontës have been cherry-picked for your awe-struck perusal.

96 Euston Road, NW1 2DB
Nearest stations: Euston, King's Cross
bl.uk

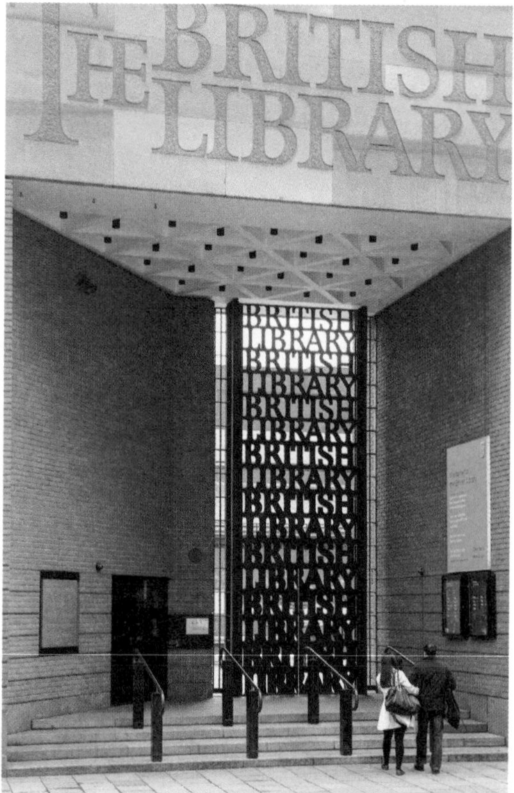
BRITISH
LIBRARY
BRITISH
LIBRARY
BRITISH
LIBRARY

28

KING'S CROSS

Culture-rich urban oasis

Two decades ago, you couldn't pay most people to brave the backstreets of King's Cross station. Thanks to a £3bn regeneration, however, this now-trendy enclave buzzes with design-conscious professionals splashing their cash at its artisan markets and hip boutiques. But you don't need a full wallet to live like a king in N1C. With a magnificent canalside nature reserve, dancing fountains on Granary Square, the tranquil Saint Pancras Gardens, captivating museums (including the Wellcome Collection [no.26]), inspiring workshops and thought-provoking art installations all completely free to access, you can enjoy an enriching day out without spending a penny.

Nearest station: King's Cross
kingscross.co.uk

29

GOD'S OWN JUNKYARD

Vintage neon nirvana

It's something of a miracle that this psychedelic Shangri-La offers free entry. With more than 1,000 illuminated signs on site, owner Matthew Bracey (son of late founder Chris) must be the recipient of one of east London's most extortionate electricity bills. But just one glimpse inside Bracey's neon museum and you can see exactly why he wants to share it with the world. Spanning seedy sex-shop signs, movie-prop neons and vintage fairground illuminations, this wacky warehouse is one of London's most dazzlingly brilliant spectacles, lending Las Vegas glitz to an industrial estate in E17 (and, you must admit, that's no mean feat).

Unit 12 Ravenswood Industrial Estate, E17 9HQ
Nearest station: Wood Street
godsownjunkyard.co.uk

30

COLUMBIA ROAD

Snowdrops and indie shops

Like lengthy lie-ins and laid-back roasts, east London's prettiest street is best enjoyed on Sundays. Only then does its famous flower market burst into bloom, filling the air with perfume, the cries of bartering barrow boys and the excited chatter of green-fingered punters bagging bargain bouquets. A purchase isn't a precondition for enjoying this iconic weekend pastime, however, with plenty of window-box inspiration to be garnered, along with more than 60 endlessly browsable independent stores – most of which are only open on market days. Break the Sunday-only rule from late November, when the legendary Wednesday carol gatherings flood the street with free Christmas cheer.

Columbia Road, E2 7RG
Nearest station: Hoxton
columbiaroad.info

31

WILLIAM MORRIS GALLERY

Victorian radical's childhood home

William Morris might be better known for his snazzy wallpaper than his poetry or socialism, but this award-winning museum – established inside his lavish family home – paints a compellingly complete picture of Walthamstow's most famous resident (that is, if you don't count Brian Harvey). Having undergone a £5m refurbishment in 2012, the sensitively modernised space boasts engaging exhibits and politically driven temporary installations which Morris himself would declare both beautiful and useful. Bypass the mildly exorbitant café and scoff your sandwiches in the pretty surrounds of Lloyd Park (once Morris's back garden) instead.

Forest Road, E17 4PP
Nearest station: Walthamstow Central
mmgallery.org.uk

INDIGO

32

WOOD STREET WALLS

Alfresco art gallery

Thought Shoreditch was London's leading street-art district? You might be due a trip to E17. Here, across two square miles, an ever-changing collection of eye-catching murals makes up what's arguably London's best (and largest) outdoor gallery – most of them facilitated by Wood Street Walls since the prolific collective was formed in 2015. Subjects and styles are diverse, spanning abstract toasters and geometric greyhounds through to a kebab shop-framing bookshelf and a rehashed baroque master-piece. Once you've exhausted E17's offerings, head south to E10 and E11 instalment, featuring a dreamy flock of birds and the community crowd-funded Walala Parade. And don't worry, you can download their free map.

Nearest station: Wood Street
woodstreetwalls.co.uk

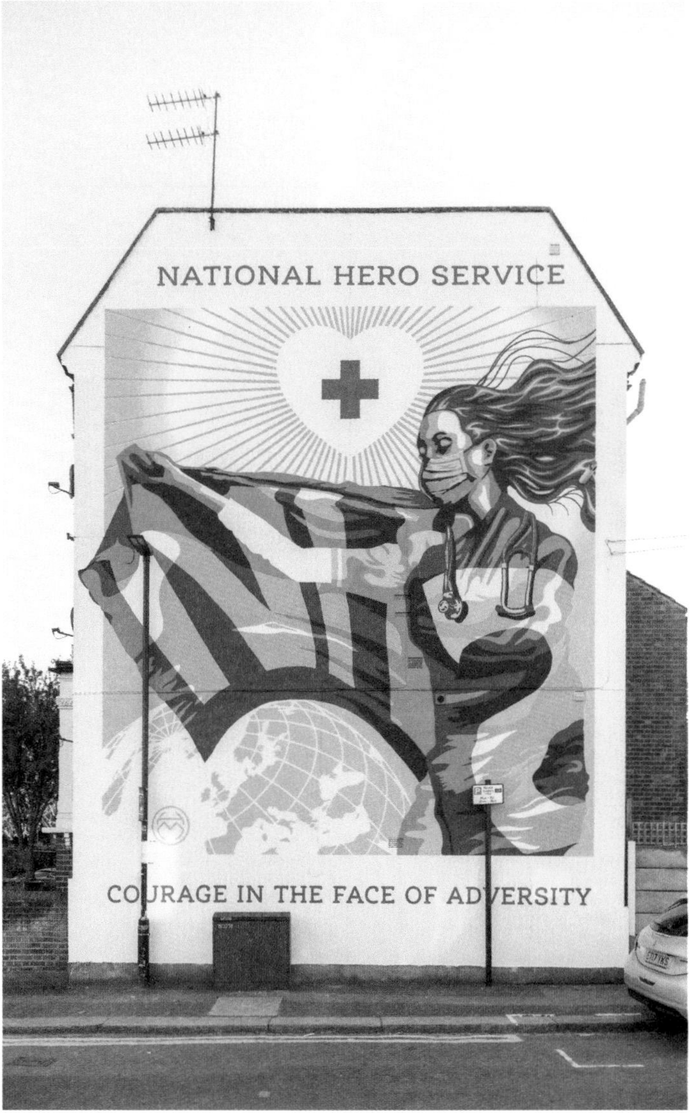
NATIONAL HERO SERVICE
COURAGE IN THE FACE OF ADVERSITY

33

MUSEUM OF THE HOME

Absorbing exhibits on domestic life

Pre-£18m facelift, Hackney's monument to domesticity felt anything but homely – a fact made even more uncomfortable by its former moniker (the Geffrye Museum), a nod to the building's slave-trading benefactor. Today, with its amended name, state-of-the-art extension and heightened focus on the diverse community it serves, the bigger, better Museum of the Home is easily one of London's most underrated free days out. In fact, its complimentary offerings are so great – its interactives so well-conceived, its gardens so scenic and temporary displays so thought-provoking – you might be able to overlook how overpriced its café is.

136 Kingsland Road, E2 8EA
Nearest station: Hoxton
museumofthehome.org.uk

34

LONGPLAYER

Singing bowls in a Victorian lighthouse

A visit to London's only lighthouse comes with a substantial side helping of existential angst, courtesy of the 1,000-year-long musical composition it houses – and the issue of upkeep the song's longevity raises. Mortal dread aside, this (now non-functioning) folly must be one of the most peaceful spots in the capital, located on the eerily remote Trinity Buoy Wharf and boasting serene Thameside vistas that are perfectly complemented by Longplayer's soothing Tibetan sound bowl-made harmonies. The composition is also available to listen to online, but the experience goes deeper than mere acoustics, and this place must be seen to be believed.

Trinity Buoy Wharf, E14 0JY
Nearest station: Canning Town
longplayer.org

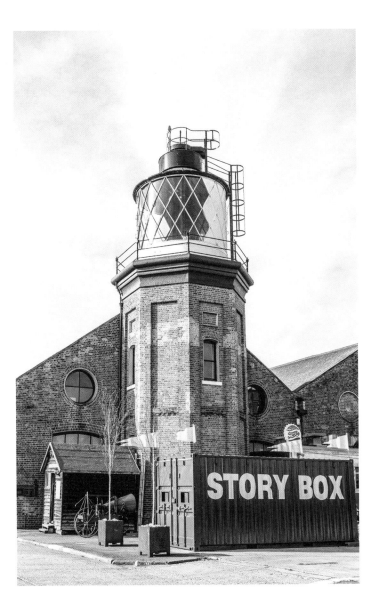

35

MUDCHUTE FARM

Donkeys in the Docklands

No matter how madly in love with urban life you are, sometimes you just can't shake the overwhelming desire to be surrounded by animals. Happily, city-dwelling livestock lovers need look no further than the capital's two-dozen city farms – most of which are totally free to visit. If we *must* pick favourites though, Mudchute's 100-strong menagerie and surreal proximity to Canary Wharf's skyscrapers means it just about clinches the top spot. Trying to convince the kids? The delightful pets' corner, weekly loose-parts play sessions and a packed calendar of free family events ought to bring the boys (and girls) to the (farm)yard.

Pier Street, E14 3HP
Nearest station: Mudchute
mudchute.org

36

THE LINE ART TRAIL

Longitudinal art walk

What links a stack of supermarket trollies, a vertical cross-section of a sand dredger and the world's tallest tunnel slide? While there's no real unifying theme to The Line's two-dozen sculptures – and even their supposed location on the meridian line can feel a bit stretched at times – joining its dots feels significantly more thrilling than your average art trail, with completion necessitating a 115m climb, numerous bridge crossings and a cable-car ride. Of course, you can visit as many or as few of the sculptures as you like, but be sure to put Rana Begum's ethereal clouds and Tracey Emin's hauntingly beautiful perching birds at the top of your list.

Queen Elizabeth Olympic Park, E20 2AD
Nearest station: Stratford
the-line.org

37

NOW GALLERY

Trailblazing art space with
mind-bending installations

While in recent years London's art scene has grown saturated with ever bigger and better immersive exhibitions – usually with the price tags to match – this Greenwich gallery has been quietly staging its own delightfully escapist, endlessly Instagrammable shows for free. A champion of young, politically driven and LGBT+ artists, NOW is renowned for its fun, inventive and refreshingly accessible exhibitions. Shows such as Camille Walala's patterned maze, Hattie Stewart's eye-popping doodleverse and Kinska's ceramic dreamscape have blown us away in the past, but we get the feeling we haven't seen anything yet.

Peninsula Square, SE10 0SQ
Nearest station: North Greenwich
nowgallery.co.uk

38

BFI MEDIATHEQUE

Encyclopaedic film archive

You could spend the rest of your life nestled inside one of BFI's cosy Mediatheque booths devouring small- and silver-screen gems, and still only ingest a fraction of what's on offer. Spanning everything from kitchen-sink dramas to cult kids' classics and heart-warming home movies to video nasties, this 95,000-title archive will make you laugh, cry and maybe even scream – although the helpful organisation by genre will ensure that it's not overwhelming. So, the next time you're in need of a little escapism, why not ditch the £15 cinema tickets and connect to the BFI's free digital jukebox instead?

Southbank Centre, Belvedere Road, SE1 8XX
Nearest station: Waterloo
bfi.org.uk

39
TATE MODERN

Celebrated contemporary art gallery

Why is the world so dotty for Kusama? What's so radical about Rothko? And what the dickens is Dada? The answers to all of these questions and many more can be found inside Britain's foremost house of modern art, where a free education awaits the Cubism-curious in the form of themed collection displays spanning early Modernism through to contemporary works by living artists, mind-blowing new commissions in the iconic Turbine Hall and arty evening entertainment at Tate Lates. While some of the paid shows are worth forking out for, most of the best bits will cost you nothing but your (well-spent) time.

Bankside, SE1 9TG
Nearest stations: Blackfriars, Southwark
Paid entry to some exhibitions
tate.org.uk

40

CHAPEL OF ST PETER & ST PAUL

Inclusive concerts in the Old Royal Naval College

Think 'hospital chapel', and something low-key and cosy might spring to mind, but this neoclassical masterpiece is anything but. Constructed as part of Sir Christopher Wren's magnificent twin-domed Royal Naval Hospital (now the aforementioned ORNC), this capacious place of prayer might feel vaguely daunting with its elaborate Rococo stylings and sometimes sinister Biblical imagery, but it's actually proudly inclusive and open to all regardless of religious inclination. Plus, it offers free weekly choral Evensong and regular lunchtime chamber concerts to anyone in need of some harmony – musically or otherwise.

College Row, SE10 9NN
Nearest station: Greenwich
ornc.org

41

LASSCO

Reclaimed relics in elegant setting

Sitting pretty on the edge of the uninspiring Vaux-hall Gyratory, this seriously upscale salvage store is, by contrast, a brimming font of interior design inspiration. Arranged across an immaculate Georgian mansion that doubles as a chic wedding venue, this Aladdin's cave of preloved gems is a million miles from your average antiques shop, showcasing everything from Victorian boot jacks and Regency doorknobs to reclaimed Louis XV beds and full-on moulded ceilings rescued from grand abodes. Take notes and as many snaps as your memory card allows – and watch out for the resident ghost bride.

Brunswick House, Wandsworth Road, SW8 2LG
Nearest station: Vauxhall
lassco.co.uk

42

CRYSTAL PALACE PARK

Ever popular Victorian pleasure ground

In its heyday, Crystal Palace Park was synonymous with innovation, famed as the permanent home of Joseph Paxton's gleaming Great Exhibition building and a menacing mob of model dinosaurs – the height of sophistication in 1854. Today, with the palace long gone and the dinosaurs long derided for their zoological inaccuracies, the 200-acre park could easily be a shadow of its illustrious former self. If anything, though, its faded grandeur and weird relics only add to its contemporary allure, and with a perplexing 150-year-old maze and that herd of derpy dinosaurs, it's still a serious candidate for south London's 'best green space'.

Thicket Road, SE19 2GA
Nearest station: Crystal Palace Park
crystalpalaceparktrust.org

43

LEAKE STREET TUNNEL

Graffiti gallery underneath Waterloo

Ok, so it's not quite the Berlin Wall, but London's longest legal graffiti wall is still an obligatory stop for street art fanatics, boasting 300 metres of ever-changing murals. Occupying a disused road tunnel under Waterloo station, this eye-poppingly colourful, refreshingly unconventional (and satisfyingly echoey) gallery was born out of Banksy's Cans Festival in 2008 and continues to entice the capital with its alternative public events programme, dramatic light shows and enlightening graffiti workshops – all of which are (you guessed it) absolutely free.

Leake Street, SE1 7NN
Nearest station: Waterloo
leakestreetarches.london

44

BOROUGH MARKET

Bustling smorgasbord of delights

If food shopping on an empty stomach is a bad idea, then surely browsing the capital's premier speciality food market on a budget is an even worse one? Well, not necessarily. While few London locations will whet your appetite quite like this world-famous foodie utopia (and it's not exactly renowned for its bargain prices), you don't need loads of dough to take advantage of its myriad pleasures. Instead, enjoy the buzzy vibes, abundant aromas, atmospheric setting, infinite people-watching opportunities, and endless meal inspiration (and perhaps even a free sample or two).

Southwark Street, SE1 1TL
Nearest station: London Bridge
boroughmarket.org.uk

45

NATIONAL THEATRE BACKSTAGE HIGH LEVEL WALKWAY

A lofty look behind the scenes

Ever wondered what it takes to pull together a world-class theatrical production? While you might not always have the funds for NT tickets, a sneak peek backstage is yours for the taking all year round, courtesy of a galleried walkway in the gods of its vast production workshops. This elevated corridor offers curious visitors a preview of everything but the performance, with chances to play *Where's Wally* with set builders, costume creators, scene painters and prop makers, as well as see some fairly bonkers objects from its ever-growing archive (severed heads, anyone?).

Upper Ground, SE1 9PX
Nearest station: Waterloo East
nationaltheatre.org.uk

46

VICTORIA & ALBERT MUSEUM

Bastion of culture in London's Museum Quarter

With blockbuster exhibitions popping up every few months and sell-out shows including *Alexander McQueen: Savage Beauty* and *David Bowie Is* in its back catalogue, it's easy to forget that the V&A is, at its core, a free resource. With more than two million objects in its possession, the world's largest museum of art and design is a virtually infinite source of inspiration – spanning costume, sculpture, interiors and everything in between. The new '1900-Now' design exhibit, famed 'Fashion' gallery, glittering 'Jewellery' room and riveting 'Rapid Response Collecting' room are all great places to start, while complimentary lunchtime lectures, live discussions and family drop-ins will leave you just as stimulated as those big-ticket retrospectives.

Cromwell Road, SW7 2RL
Nearest station: South Kensington
vam.ac.uk

47

NATURAL HISTORY MUSEUM

Dinosaurs and dodos

This labyrinthine museum's freeness can feel like a curse – to the extent that you might happily pay for your visit if it meant not feeling like a sardine for the duration. The most popular exhibits (we're looking at you, animatronic T-Rex) are reliably packed every day of the week, but there's plenty more to discover across this vast cathedral of nature, from the explosive 'From the Beginning' gallery to the fascinating 'Treasures' room – a real hidden gem. Keep an eye out for the reopening of the five-acre gardens, set to feature a 'Walk Through Deep Time' with its own towering Diplodocus – which should take the pressure off the T-Rex, at the very least.

Cromwell Road, SW7 5BD
Nearest station: South Kensington
Book in advance
nhm.ac.uk

48

DESIGN MUSEUM

Objectively brilliant exhibits

Many of the heftier exhibitions put on by Holland Park's shrine to design require a similarly hefty sum to enter, but don't be deterred. The museum's free displays change regularly and most warrant a trip west all by themselves, with recent hits including Camille Walala's shoppable 'Supermarket' installation where you could browse everyday household items designed by a host of young artists. Elsewhere, the permanent 'Designer Maker User' gallery offers an eye-catching insight into the history of design, and the impeccably curated shop is always worth a browse, even if your budget is non-existent.

224-238 Kensington High Street, w8 6AG
Nearest station: High Street Kensington
designmuseum.org

49

SCIENCE MUSEUM

Colossal showcase of human ingenuity

So vast is this South Kensington institution, you could probably squeeze at least three daytrips out of its free galleries alone. Assuming you're only planning the one, head straight for the 'Exploring Space' exhibit for a stellar introduction to interplanetary travel, before delving into object galleries spanning flight, engineering and scientific innovation (the delightfully narcissistic 'Who Am I?' is a favourite). Visiting with kids? The teen-focused 'Technicians' gallery and preschool-perfect 'The Garden' play space are both free to access and satisfyingly hands-on – though the rather dated latter might benefit from some of those scientific innovations.

Exhibition Road, SW7 2DD
Nearest station: South Kensington
Book in advance
sciencemuseum.org.uk

Birth of the
modern airliner.
↑

Transforming
the Wellcome Wing

50

TATE BRITAIN

Winter lights and Pre-Raphaelites

Having garnered a reputation as the staid older sibling of the Tate Modern, Tate's Millbank outpost tends to be the somewhat quieter of the two galleries, though its offerings – particularly the free ones – are arguably superior. With recent Duveen Gallery exhibits comprising Heather Phillipson's immersive alien universe and Anthea Hamilton's dancing squash, winter commissions including a festival of neon and giant glowing slugs, not to mention an open-access family studio and killer permanent collection with Waterhouse's *Lady of Shalott* and Millais' *Ophelia*, this Pimlico palace might just be (whisper it) our favourite London gallery.

Millbank, SW1P 4RG
Nearest station: Pimlico
tate.org.uk

51

WALLACE COLLECTION

Treasure trove of decorative arts

You may never bag that dream home in Marylebone, but a gratuitous snoop around the sumptuous former residence of the marquesses of Hertford might just be the next best thing. Here, visitors can eye up everything from fine French furniture to priceless paintings by the likes of Titian, Van Dyck and Rembrandt – either at their own pace or as part of an illuminating free tour. Costly medieval and Renaissance objects, foreboding weaponry and some impressively elaborate historical armour complete this remarkably un-touristy museum's arsenal (and you can even try on a suit, if you like).

Manchester Square, W1U 3BN
Nearest station: Bond Street
wallacecollection.org

52

HYDE PARK & KENSINGTON GARDENS

Spellbinding green space

Anyone who's ever strolled through Hyde Park's tree-lined avenues or wandered Kensington Gardens' meandering paths will vouch for the fairy-tale magic of this 600-acre site. While the latter served as the inspiration for J.M. Barrie's Peter Pan, a character immortalised by the Gardens' fairy-adorned bronze statue, the former possesses its own charms – from haunting memorials to lively public addresses at Speakers' Corner. Elsewhere, the trailblazing Serpentine galleries are free to enter, while the brilliant Pan-themed playground and mischievous play fountain – both dedicated to the late Princess of Wales – will leave you wishing you'd never grown up.

West Carriage Drive, w2 2UH
Nearest stations: Hyde Park Corner, Lancaster Gate
royalparks.org.uk

53

ST JAMES'S PARK

Grandiose gardens overlooking Buckingham Palace

London's oldest Royal Park is so jaw-droppingly grand, a ramble around its 57 acres feels other-worldly. Majestic palaces, pouch-billed pelicans and a chocolate-box cottage (actually the offices of the London Historic Parks and Gardens Trust) are just a few of its scenic delights, and its famous Blue Bridge is probably one of the most photographed spots in London. The almost daily Changing of the Guard ceremonies are free to watch outside the palace, as is the similarly hypnotic (but much less frequent) Trooping the Colour, though the latter requires an eye-wateringly early start to bag a good spot. Bringing the kids? The palace view playground is worth battling the crowds for.

SW1A 2BJ
Nearest station: St James's Park
royalparks.org.uk

54

FRIDAY NIGHT SKATE & SUNDAY STROLL

Mobile roller disco

Bored stiff by sightseeing buses and walking tours? These long-running marshalled skate-meets offer a dramatically different way to explore the city, whether you sign up for the fast-paced Friday night frolic or the slightly more sluggish Sunday amble. Two-hour jaunts cover up to 15 miles and can attract some (ahem) *wheel* talent, so make sure you're at least vaguely confident on eight wheels (it is BYO-skates) before lacing up and tagging along. Once you're prepped, take advantage of traffic-free roads, banging tunes (the organisers bring speakers) and a massive gang of ready-made mates on skates.

Skates start at Wellington Arch at 8pm on Fridays
and on Serpentine Road at 2pm on Sundays.
Nearest station: Hyde Park Corner
lfns.co.uk

55

LITTLE VENICE

Picturesque canal-side festivities

Aside from its abundance of canals, Little Venice is nothing like big Venice. What it lacks in Byzantine palaces and stripy-shirted gondoliers, however, this watery enclave in Westminster compensates for with colourful narrowboats, stuccoed townhouses and postcard-worthy views. It's also very easy to have a free day out here (which is more than can be said for its extortionate namesake), with free events including screenings at Sheldon Square Amphitheatre and the well-loved annual Canalway Cavalcade. Alternatively, you could just enjoy a leisurely stroll up the towpath, where you might even be lucky enough to spot a paddleboarder or two – who look just like gondoliers, if you squint.

Blomfield Road, W9 2PF
Nearest station: Warwick Avenue
canalrivertrust.org.uk

56

HOGARTH'S HOUSE

Atmospheric abode of the satirical artist

Imagining Hogarth's Chiswick home as the 'little country box' he moved into in 1749 is a bit of a stretch nearly 300 years later with the A4 roaring past, and yet the artist's presence remains so potent you half expect to find his ghost creaking around in an upstairs bedroom. While the villa's contents are fairly sparse in terms of Hogarth's worldly possessions, most of its features are original, with charmingly low doorways and noisy, sloping floorboards amping up the ambience. And while you've probably seen the artist's best-known works a hundred times before, you'll agree they're at their most evocative hanging on the wonky walls of the rooms in which they were conceived.

Hogarth Lane, Great West Road, W4 2QN
Nearest stations: Chiswick, Stamford Brook
hogarthshouse.org

57

SERVICES AT WESTMINSTER ABBEY

Spellbinding rituals at a historic royal church

Coronations, royal weddings and the tombs of celebrated poets: Westminster Abbey's claims to fame are so extraordinary, it's easy to forget that it's still a working church – and that you can attend any one of its peaceful daily services completely free of charge. While you needn't be a practising Christian to experience the magic of the Abbey's legendary evensong, or even to observe the solemnity of Holy Communion, you will be expected to sit relatively still for the duration – and ushered out pretty sharpish when it ends. So don't assume you'll be getting the grand tour on your way out (for that, you'll need to cough up the fairly hefty admission fee).

20 Deans Yard, SW1P 3PA
Nearest station: Westminster
westminster-abbey.org

58

SOTHEBY'S AUCTION HOUSE

Hammer time at this Mayfair institution

In need of some drama but don't fancy the theatre? Sotheby's public auctions offer all the excitement of the stage and then some, with the chance to eyeball prominent artworks, witness nail-biting bidding wars and make believe you're a billionaire art collector without so much as lifting a paddle. Upcoming auctions are listed online, and you can opt to be alerted should your favourite artist's work come to market – though the highly charged atmosphere and lively bidding action should be enough to entice you, whatever the lot. As for inadvertent bids... all potential bidders must register beforehand *and* show proof of assets, so you can't accidentally bag a Banksy, twitchy arm or not.

34-35 New Bond Street, W1A 2AA
Nearest station: Bond Street
sothebys.com

59

HOUSES OF PARLIAMENT PUBLIC GALLERIES

Eavesdrop on the jeers and 'hear, hears'

Ever fantasised about being a fly on the wall in the Palace of Westminster? While you might not be privy to much backbench gossip up in the gods of the House of Commons, sitting in on parliamentary debates still feels wickedly nosy. Tickets to PMQs are free but relatively hard to come by, as prime-ministerial grillings are often more gripping than an episode of Borgen. So, badger your MP (or even just try your luck on the day). Just leave any eggs or flour-filled balloons at home – and prepare yourself for a pretty thorough frisk beforehand.

Palace of Westminster, SW1A 0AA
Nearest station: Westminster
Book in advance
parliament.uk

IMAGE CREDITS

God's Own Junkyard (all images) ©Roger Garfield / Alamy Stock Photo; The Garden at 120 (pp.4–5) © Steve Tulley / Alamy Stock Photo; Sir John Soanes's Museum © Gareth Gardner / Sir John Soanes's Museum; BAPS Shri Swaminarayan Mandir, Barbican, British Museum, Design Museum © Taran Wilkhu Photography; Hampstead Heath (p.8) © Robert Stainforth / Alamy Stock Photo; Crystal Palace Park (p.9) © Andreas Lostromos @meletispix; Old Bailey © SOPA Images / Dave Rushen; LSE Public Lectures © London School of Economics / Guy Jordan 2018; Old Blue Last © Roberto Herrett / Alamy Stock Photo; Guildhall Art Gallery (first image) © Lewis Buchan / Alamy Stock Photo; Guildhall Art Gallery (second image) © Nick Harrison / Alamy Stock Photo; National Gallery (first image) © Kamira / Alamy Stock Photo; National Gallery (second image) © National Gallery; Gresham College © Liam Pearson @lundonlens / Gresham College; Tara Yoga Centre © Tara Yoga Centre; Inner Space © Inner Space-Brahma Kumaris; Grant Museum of Zoology © Peter Macdiarmid / Getty Images; St Dunstan in the East, The Garden at 120, Parkland Walk, Mudchute Farm, Crystal Palace Park, Hyde Park and Kensington Gardens, St James's Park © Marco Kesseler; St Paul's Cathedral (first image) © Taran Wilkhu Photography; St Paul's Cathedral (second image) © B. O'Kane / Alamy Stock Photo; St Paul's Cathedral (third image) © John Michaels / Alamy Stock Photo; London Mithraeum © John Edwards / Alamy Stock Photo; Architectural Association School of Architecture © Martin Usbourne; Royal Opera House (first image) © Ian Dagnall / Alamy Stock Photo; Royal Opera House (second image) © Laura Aziz / 2019 ROH; Hampstead Heath (first image) © Michael Heath / Alamy Stock Photo; Hampstead Heath (second image) © Lee Martin / Alamy Stock Photo; Abney Park Cemetery © Beca Jones; UCL Observatory © Simon Stapley / Alamy Stock Photo; Kenwood House (first image) © English Heritage; Kenwood House (second image) © Taran Wilkhu Photography; Royal Academy of Music © Adam Scott; Wellcome Collection © Tony French / Alamy Stock Photo; Wood Street Walls © Tim Crooker 2023 / artwork by Holy Moly @holymoly; British Library (first image) © Barbara West / Alamy Stock Photo; British Library (second image) © Reiner Elsen / Alamy Stock Photo; British Library (third image) © Jo Chambers / Alamy Stock Photo; King's Cross © Monica Wells / Alamy Stock Photo; Columbia Road © Ben Speck / Alamy Stock Photo; William Morris Gallery (first image) © Victoria Penrose-Jones; William Morris Gallery (second image) © Charlotte Schreiber; Museum of the Home (first image) © Loop Images Ltd / Alamy Stock Photo; Museum of Home (second image) © Jane Lloyd; Museum of the Home (third image) © Museum of the Home; Longplayer (first and fourth image) © Nathaniel Noir / Alamy Stock Photo; Longplayer (second image) © James Whitaker; Longplayer (third image) © Charlotte Schreiber; The Line Art Trail, Rana Begum, Catching Colour, 2022 © Angus Mills / Rana Begum; Now Gallery © Nathaniel Noir / Alamy Stock Photo; BFI © BFI. Photography: Gareth Gardner; Tate Modern (first image) © Audrey Eberhard / Alamy Stock Photo; Tate Modern (second image) © godrick / Alamy Stock Photo; Chapel of St Paul and St Peter (first image) © Old Royal Naval College; LASSCO © Lesley Lau; Leake Street Arches © Jansos / Alamy Stock Photo; Borough Market © Red Agency commissioned by Borough Market; National Theatre © Nathaniel Noir / Alamy Stock Photo; Victoria and Albert Museum (first image) © Victoria and Albert Museum, London; Victoria and Albert Museum (second image) © Vivienne Westwood; Victoria and Albert Museum (third image) © www.alanwilliamsphotography.com; Natural History Museum © Trustees of the Natural History Museum; Science Museum © Michael Kemp / Alamy Stock Photo; Tate Britain (first image) © Guy Bell / Alamy Stock Photo; Tate Britain © Alex Segre / Alamy Stock Photo; The Wallace Collection © Alison Wright; Friday Night Skate & Sunday Stroll © John Bracegirdle / Alamy Stock Photo; Little Venice © RJT Photography / Alamy Stock Photo; Hogarth's House © Lizetta Lyster; Westminster Abbey (first image) © John Michaels / Alamy Stock Photo; Westminster Abbey (second image) © Michael Matthews / Alamy Stock Photo; Sotheby's © Jeff Gilbert / Alamy Stock Photo; Houses of Parliament (first image) © Andrew Michael / Alamy Stock Photo; Houses of Parliament (second image) © UK Parliament.

CONTRIBUTORS

Emmy Watts is a Yorkshire-born writer who has authored or co-authored four other books in this series, including *An Opinionated Guide to Eco London*. She's got pretty good at living frugally in the 14 years she's lived in London, even if her two young daughters are doing their best to put a stop to that.

Hoxton Mini Press is a small indie publisher based in east London. We make books about London (and beyond) with a dedication to lovely, sustainable production and brilliant photography. When we started the company, people told us 'print was dead'; we wanted to prove them wrong. Books are no longer about information but objects in their own right: things to collect and own and inspire. We are an environmentally conscious publisher, committed to offsetting our carbon footprint. This book, for instance, is 100 percent carbon compensated, with offset purchased from Stand for Trees.

INDEX

Abney Park Cemetery, 20

Architectural Association Public Programme, 16

BAPS Shri Swaminarayan Mandir, 24

Barbican Conservatory, 13

BFI Mediatheque, 38

Borough Market, 44

British Library, 27

British Museum, 2

Chapel of St Peter & St Paul, 40

Columbia Road, 30

Crystal Palace Park, 42

Design Museum, 48

Evensong at St Paul's Cathedral, 14

Friday Night Skate & Sunday Stroll, 54

God's Own Junkyard, 29

Grant Museum of Zoology, 11

Gresham College Lectures, 8

Guildhall Art Gallery, 6

Hampstead Heath, 19

Hatha Yoga at Tara Yoga Centre, 9

Hogarth's House, 56

Houses of Parliament Public Galleries, 59

Hyde Park & Kensington Gardens, 52

Inner Space, 10

Kenwood House, 22

King's Cross, 28

LASSCO, 41

Leake Street Tunnel, 43

Little Venice, *55*

Live at Lunch at the Royal Opera House, *17*

London Mithraeum, *15*

Longplayer, *34*

LSE Public Lectures, *3*

Mudchute Farm, *35*

Museum of the Home, *33*

National Theatre Backstage High Level Walkway, *45*

Natural History Museum, *47*

NOW Gallery, *37*

Old Bailey Trial, *1*

Parkland Walk, *23*

Royal Academy of Music, *25*

Science Museum, *49*

Services at Westminster Abbey, *57*

Sir John Soane's Museum, *4*

Sotheby's Auction House, *58*

St Dunstan in the East, *12*

St James's Park, *53*

Tate Britain, *50*

Tate Modern, *39*

The Garden at 120, *18*

The Line Art Trail, *36*

The National Gallery, *7*

The Old Blue Last Free Gigs, *5*

Wallace Collection, *51*

Wellcome Collection, *26*

UCL Observatory, *21*

Victoria & Albert museum, *46*

William Morris Gallery, *31*

Wood Street Walls, *32*

An Opinionated Guide to Free London
First edition

Published in 2023 by Hoxton Mini Press, London
Copyright © Hoxton Mini Press 2023. All rights reserved.

Text by Emmy Watts
Copy-editing by Octavia Stocker
Design by Richard Mason
Production by Sarah-Louise Deazley
Production and editorial support by Alison Evans and Georgia Williams

With thanks to Matthew Young for initial series design.

Please note: we recommend checking the websites listed for each
entry before you visit for the latest information on price, opening times
and pre-booking requirements.

The right of Emmy Watts to be identified as the creator of this Work has been
asserted under the Copyright, Designs and Patents Act 1988.

A CIP catalogue record for this book is available from the British Library.

ISBN: 978-1-914314-32-2

Printed and bound by OZGraf, Poland

Hoxton Mini Press is an environmentally conscious publisher, committed
to offsetting our carbon footprint. This book is 100 percent carbon
compensated, with offset purchased from Stand For Trees.

For every book you buy from our website, we plant a tree:
www.hoxtonminipress.com